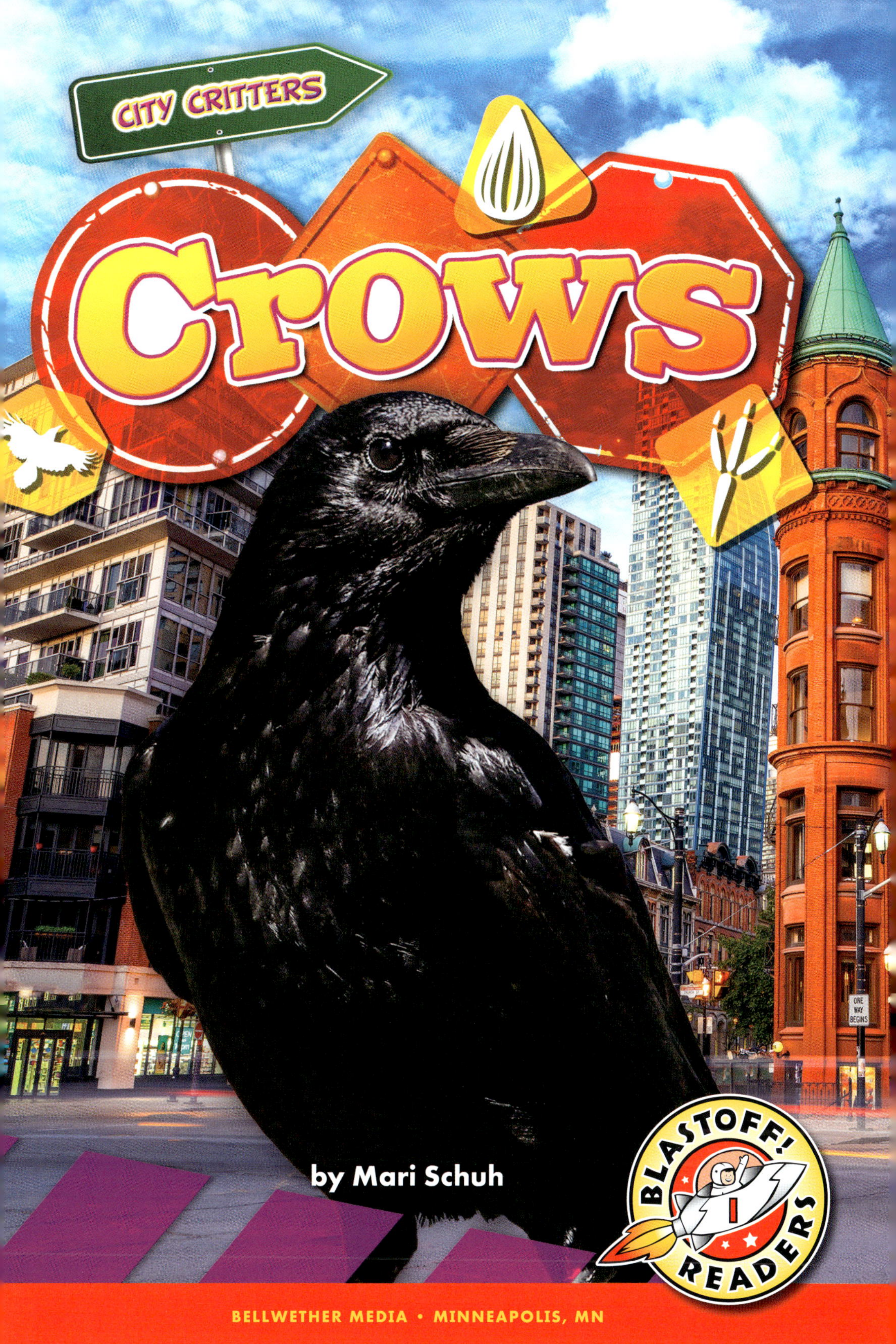
CITY CRITTERS
Crows
by Mari Schuh
BLASTOFF! READERS
1
ONE WAY BEGINS
BELLWETHER MEDIA • MINNEAPOLIS, MN

Blastoff! Readers are carefully developed by literacy experts to build reading stamina and move students toward fluency by combining standards-based content with developmentally appropriate text.

Level 1 provides the most support through repetition of high-frequency words, light text, predictable sentence patterns, and strong visual support.

Level 2 offers early readers a bit more challenge through varied sentences, increased text load, and text-supportive special features.

Level 3 advances early-fluent readers toward fluency through increased text load, less reliance on photos, advancing concepts, longer sentences, and more complex special features.

★ Blastoff! Universe

Reading Level

Blastoff! Beginners — Grade K

Blastoff! Readers — Grades 1–3

Blastoff! Discovery — Grade 4

This edition first published in 2026 by Bellwether Media, Inc.

Library of Congress Cataloging-in-Publication Data

LC record for Crows available at: https://lccn.loc.gov/2025012861

Editor: Betsy Rathburn   Designer: Gabriel Hilger

Printed in the United States of America, North Mankato, MN.

Table of Contents

What Are Crows?

Crows are smart birds. Many live in cities. They fly through parks and parking lots.

Common City Crows
American crow
carrion crow
hooded crow

Crows are big birds. Most are black. Some have white **feathers**.

feathers

Crows have long legs. They have strong **beaks**.

beak
legs

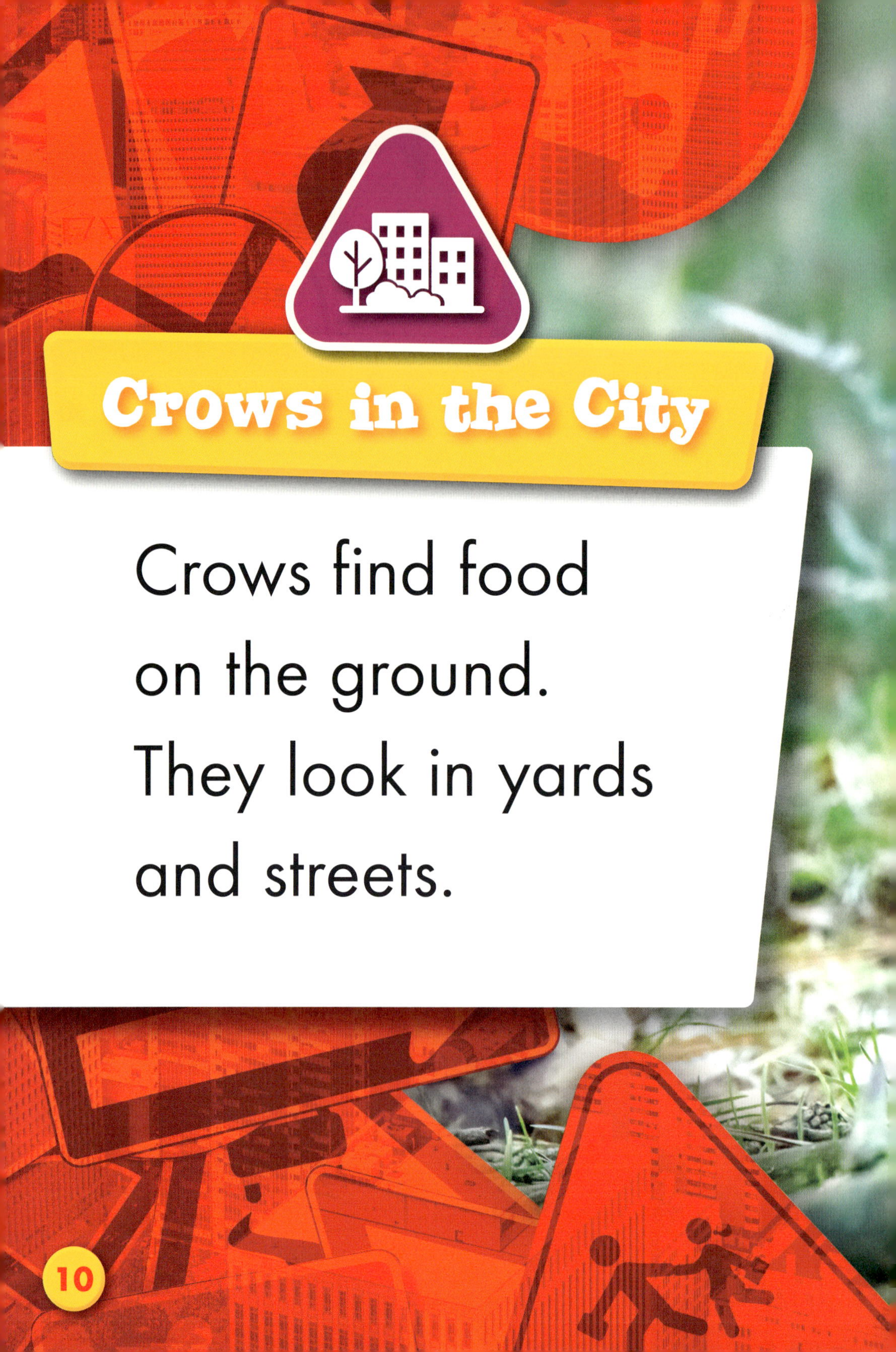

Crows in the City

Crows find food on the ground. They look in yards and streets.

Crows eat fruit, nuts, and **insects**. Some eat trash!

Crow Food
fruit
nuts
insects

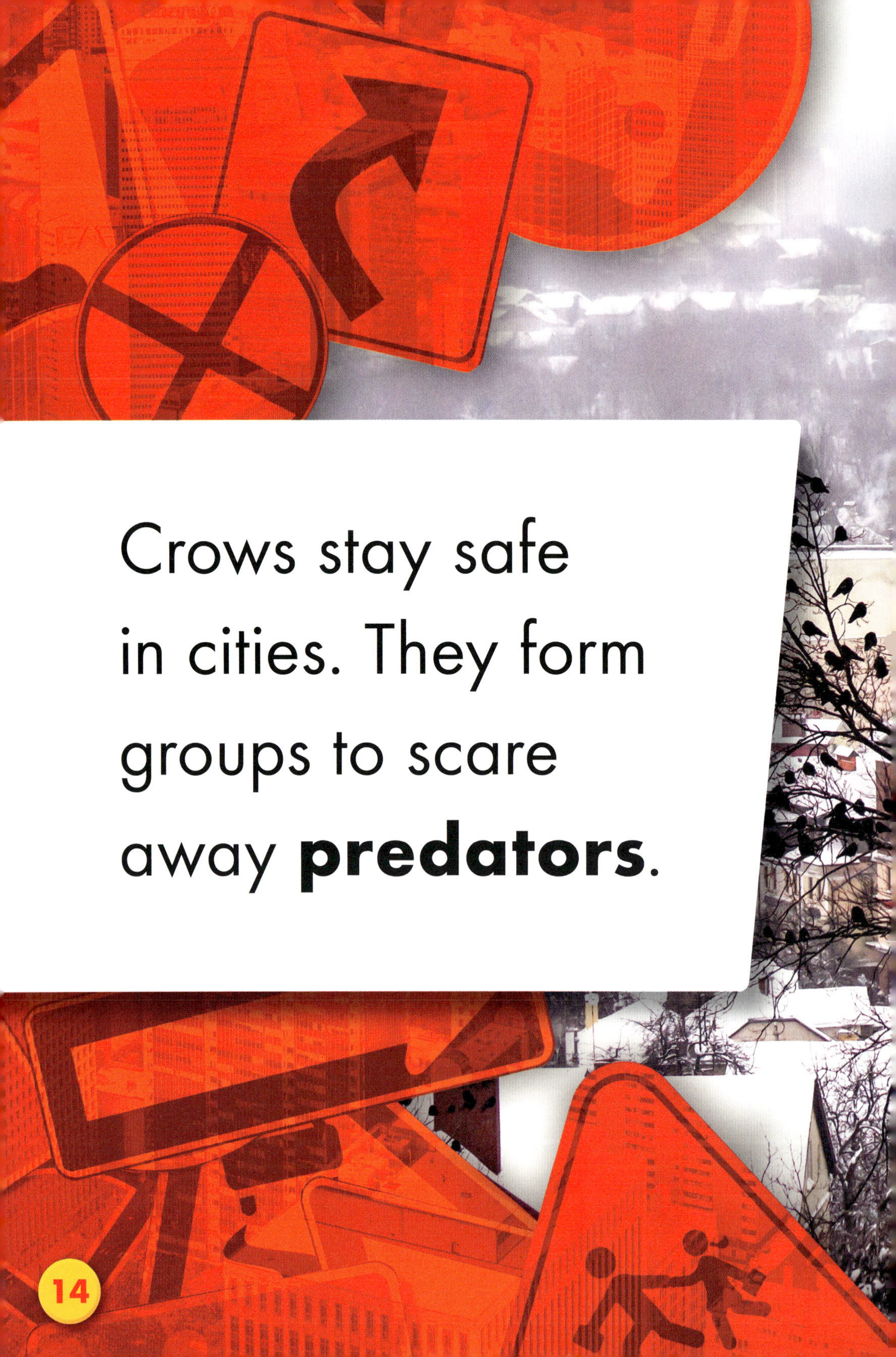

Crows stay safe in cities. They form groups to scare away **predators**.

predator

Crows often rest in groups. Groups **roost** on bridges, rooftops, and tree branches.

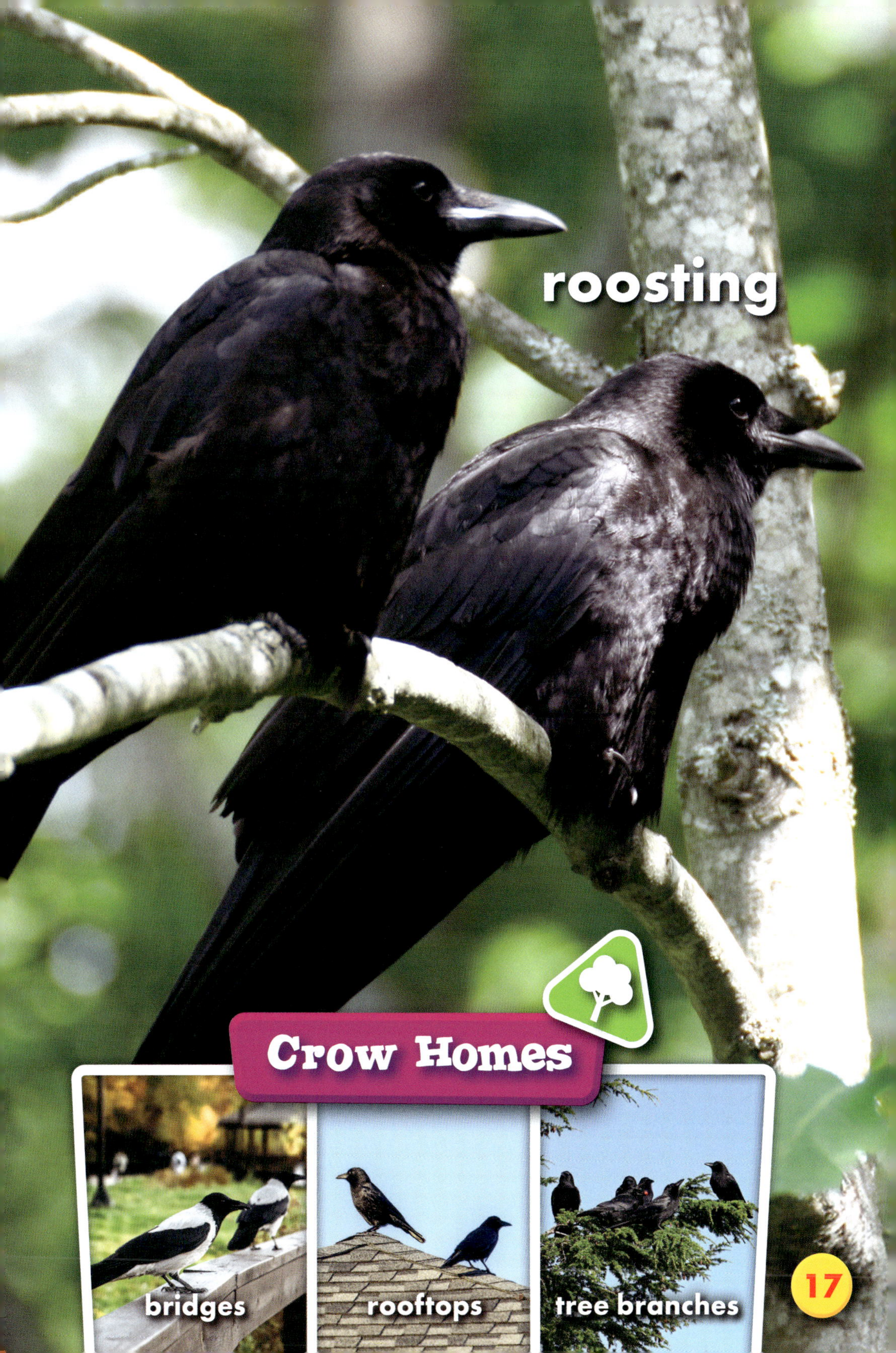
roosting
Crow Homes
bridges
rooftops
tree branches

Crows and People

Crows are loud! They bother some people. Other people like to feed them.

Some crows steal people's food. These smart birds live well in cities!

Glossary

beaks

the hard front parts of the mouths of birds

predators

animals that hunt other animals for food

feathers

light, soft coverings on birds' bodies

roost

to rest in high places

insects

small animals with six legs and hard outer bodies

To Learn More

AT THE LIBRARY

Barnes, Rachael. *Crows*. Minneapolis, Minn.: Bellwether Media, 2023.

Pang, Ursula. *Crows*. Buffalo, N.Y.: PowerKids Press, 2025.

Rice, Jamie. *Crow or Raven?* Minneapolis, Minn.: Jump!, 2023.

ON THE WEB

FACTSURFER

Factsurfer.com gives you a safe, fun way to find more information.

1. Go to www.factsurfer.com.
2. Enter "crows" into the search box and click 🔍.
3. Select your book cover to see a list of related content.

Index

The images in this book are reproduced through the courtesy of: Edwin Butter, front cover (crow); f11photo, front cover (city); Eric Isselée, p. 3; thelittlecactus, pp. 4-5; Richard Wright/ Danita Delimont, p. 5 (American crow); Eric, p. 5 (carrion crow); Grzegorz, p. 5 (hooded crow); Marcin Perkowski, pp. 6-7, 22 (feathers); Mny-Jhee, pp. 8-9; Sarah, pp. 10-11; carstenbrandt, pp. 12-13; Sappheiros, p. 13 (fruit); Valentina Shilkina, p. 13 (nuts); Aloisia, p. 13 (insects); askaternoy, pp. 14-15; Jim, p. 15 (predator); Trevor Allen, pp. 16-17; Arina Surovenko, p. 17 (bridges); knelson20, p. 17 (rooftops); JT Fisherman, p. 17 (tree branches); Light Purveyor/ Alamy Stock Photo, pp. 18-19; Colombe Photographie, pp. 20-21; Rudmer Zwerver, p. 22 (beaks); cwieders, p. 22 (insects); Bai, p. 22 (predators); Hanjo Hellmann, p. 22 (roost).